Hayley Squi

Vera Vera V̶̶

T0249250

B L O O M S B U R Y

LONDON · NEW DELHI · NEW YORK · SYDNEY

Bloomsbury Methuen Drama

An imprint of Bloomsbury Publishing Plc

50 Bedford Square
London
WC1B 3DP
UK

1385 Broadway
New York
NY 10018
USA

www.bloomsbury.com

Bloomsbury is a registered trade mark of Bloomsbury Publishing Plc

First published 2012
Reprinted 2013

Visit www.bloomsbury.com to find out more about our authors and their books
You will find extracts, author interviews, author events and you can sign up for
newsletters to be the first to hear about our latest releases and special offers.

British Library Cataloguing-in-Publication Data
A catalogue record for this book is available from the British Library.

ISBN: PB: 978-1-4081-7271-1
ePDF: 978-1-4081-7273-5
ePUB: 978-1-4081-7272-8

Library of Congress Cataloging-in-Publication Data
A catalog record for this book is available from the Library of Congress.

ROYAL COURT

The Royal Court Theatre presents

VERA VERA VERA

by **Hayley Squires**

Vera Vera Vera was first performed at The Royal Court Jerwood Theatre Upstairs, Sloane Square, on Thursday 22nd March 2012.

Principal Sponsor

VERA VERA VERA

by Hayley Squires

Emily **Danielle Flett**
Lee **Daniel Kendrick**
Danny **Tommy McDonnell**
Charlie **Abby Rakic-Platt**
Sammy **Ted Riley**

Director **Jo McInnes**
Designer **Tom Piper**
Lighting Designer **Stephen Andrews**
Sound Designer **David McSeveney**
Casting Director **Amy Ball**
Assistant Director **Ben Sayle**
Production Manager **Tariq Rifaat**
Stage Managers **Julia Slienger, Laura Draper**
Stage Management Work Placement **Elizabeth Theodora**
Set Builders **Object Construction**
Scenic Work **Jodie Pritchard**

The Royal Court and Stage Management wish to thank the following for their help with this production: Sian Gousen at SPVA, Robert Rowntree, Sean Mallet, The Sittingbourne Community College and Dr Barry Albin.

THE COMPANY

HAYLEY SQUIRES (Writer)

Hayley trained as an actor and graduated from Rose Bruford College in 2012. Vera Vera Vera is her first full-length play.

STEPHEN ANDREWS (Lighting Designer)

AS ASSOCIATE LIGHTING DESIGNER FOR THE ROYAL COURT: Jerusalem (&West End/Broadway); Enron (&West End); Clybourne Park (&West End); The Seagull (&Broadway).

AS LIGHTING DESIGNER, THEATRE INCLUDES: The Golden Dragon (ATC/Theatre Royal Plymouth/UK Tour/India/Iraq).

DANIELLE FLETT (Emily)

THEATRE INCLUDES: Burnt Oak (Leicester Square Theatre).

DANIEL KENDRICK (Lee)

THEATRE INCLUDES: Chapel Street (Old Red Lion); Coalition (Theatre 503); Rosie & Jim (The Old Market).

TELEVISION INCLUDES: EastEnders, 999.

FILM INCLUDES: Offender, Love Bites, Ghost, Katy B Easy Please Me.

RADIO INCLUDES: Caged.

TOMMY McDONNELL (Danny)

THEATRE INCLUDES: Cause Célèbre (Old Vic).

TELEVISION INCLUDES: Law & Order, Garrow's Law.

FILM INCLUDES: Piggy, St George's Day.

JO McINNES (Director)

FOR THE ROYAL COURT: Red Bud.

OTHER THEATRE INCLUDES: Marine Parade (Brighton International Festival); Christmas (Brighton Dome/Bush); Tape (New Venture Theatre, Brighton); Kaleidoshow (The Old Market).

TELEVISION & FILM INCLUDES: Pornography, The Verdict.

DAVID McSEVENEY (Sound Designer)

David trained at the Central School of Speech and Drama completing a BA (Hons) in Theatre Practice (Sound Design).

FOR THE ROYAL COURT: Constellations, The Village Bike, Clybourne Park (& West End), Ingredient X, Posh, Disconnect, Cock, A Miracle, The Stone, Shades, Seven Jewish Children, The Girlfriend Experience (&Theatre Royal Plymouth/Young Vic), Contractions, Fear and Misery/War and Peace.

OTHER THEATRE INCLUDES: Stones in His Pockets (Tricycle); Victoria Station/One for the Road (Print Room & Young Vic); On the Record (Arcola); The Tin Horizon (Theatre503); Gaslight (Old Vic); Charley's Aunt, An Hour and a Half Late (Theatre Royal Bath); A Passage to India, After Mrs Rochester, Madame Bovary (Shared Experience); Men Should Weep, Rookery Nook (Oxford Stage Company); Othello (Southwark Playhouse).

AS SOUND ASSISTANT DESIGNER: The Permanent Way (Out of Joint); My Brilliant Divorce, Auntie and Me (West End); Accidental Death of an Anarchist (Donmar).

David is Head of Sound at the Royal Court.

TOM PIPER (Designer)

FOR THE ROYAL COURT: Goodbye to All That, Backpay, Cockroach, Who?

THEATRE INCLUDES: Much Ado About Nothing, Macbeth, City Madam, Richard II, Henry IV – Parts I and II, Henry V, Henry VI – Parts I, II and III, Richard III, As You Like It, The Grain Store, The Drunks, Antony and Cleopatra (RSC); Richard III, The Tempest, As You Like It (BAM/Old Vic); Zorro (West End/Paris/Moscow/Amsterdam/Tokyo); Dealer's Choice (Menier/West End); Falstaff (Scottish Opera); Fall (Traverse); Spyski (Lyric Hammersmith & tour); The Scarecrow and His Servant (Southwark Playhouse); The Plough and the Stars, The Crucible, Six Characters in Search of an Author (Abbey, Dublin).

AWARDS INCLUDE: 2009 Olivier Award for Best Costume Design for Richard III.

Tom is the Associate Designer at the RSC.

ABBY RAKIC-PLATT (Charlie)

THEATRE INCLUDES: Burying Your Brother in the Pavement (Young Actors' Theatre).

TELEVISION INCLUDES: The Bill, The Inspector Lynley Mysteries, Murder in Mind, The Story of Tracy Beaker, Seven Wonders of the Industrial World, Bo Selecta.

FILM INCLUDES: Tracy Beaker's Movie of Me, A Small Town Duet, First Kiss.

TED RILEY (Sammy)

THEATRE INCLUDES: Grandfathers (Oval House); Aladdin (Lyric Hammersmith).

BEN SAYLE (Assistant Director)

AS A DIRECTOR, THEATRE INCLUDES: The History Boys, Dealer's Choice, The Dumb Waiter (HonesThieves).

AS AN ACTOR, THEATRE INCLUDES: Frank Incensed (Frying Camel); Eclipse (National).

APPLAUDING
THE EXCEPTIONAL.

Coutts is proud to sponsor the Royal Court Theatre

THE ENGLISH STAGE COMPANY
AT THE ROYAL COURT THEATRE

'For me the theatre is really a religion or way of life. You must decide what you feel the world is about and what you want to say about it, so that everything in the theatre you work in is saying the same thing … A theatre must have a recognisable attitude. It will have one, whether you like it or not.'

George Devine, first artistic director of the English Stage Company: notes for an unwritten book.

photo: Stephen Cummiskey

As Britain's leading national company dedicated to new work, the Royal Court Theatre produces new plays of the highest quality, working with writers from all backgrounds, and addressing the problems and possibilities of our time.

"The Royal Court has been at the centre of British cultural life for the past 50 years, an engine room for new writing and constantly transforming the theatrical culture." Stephen Daldry

Since its foundation in 1956, the Royal Court has presented premieres by almost every leading contemporary British playwright, from John Osborne's Look Back in Anger to Caryl Churchill's A Number and Tom Stoppard's Rock 'n' Roll. Just some of the other writers to have chosen the Royal Court to premiere their work include Edward Albee, John Arden, Richard Bean, Samuel Beckett, Edward Bond, Leo Butler, Jez Butterworth, Martin Crimp, Ariel Dorfman, Stella Feehily, Christopher Hampton, David Hare, Eugène Ionesco, Ann Jellicoe, Terry Johnson, Sarah Kane, David Mamet, Martin McDonagh, Conor McPherson, Joe Penhall, Lucy Prebble, Mark Ravenhill, Simon Stephens, Wole Soyinka, Polly Stenham, David Storey, debbie tucker green, Arnold Wesker and Roy Williams.

"It is risky to miss a production there." Financial Times

In addition to its full-scale productions, the Royal Court also facilitates international work at a grass roots level, developing exchanges which bring young writers to Britain and sending British writers, actors and directors to work with artists around the world. The research and play development arm of the Royal Court Theatre, The Studio, finds the most exciting and diverse range of new voices in the UK. The Studio runs play-writing groups including the Young Writers Programme, Critical Mass for black, Asian and minority ethnic writers and the biennial Young Writers Festival. For further information, go to www.royalcourttheatre.com/playwriting/the-studio.

"Yes, the Royal Court is on a roll. Yes, Dominic Cooke has just the genius and kick that this venue needs… It's fist-bitingly exciting." Independent

ROYAL COURT SUPPORTERS

The Royal Court is able to offer its unique playwriting and audience development programmes because of significant and longstanding partnerships with the organisations that support it.

Coutts is the Principal Sponsor of the Royal Court. The Genesis Foundation supports the Royal Court's work with International Playwrights. Theatre Local is sponsored by Bloomberg. The Jerwood Charitable Foundation supports new plays by playwrights through the Jerwood New Playwrights series. Over the past ten years the BBC has supported the Gerald Chapman Fund for directors.

The Harold Pinter Playwright's Award is given annually by his widow, Lady Antonia Fraser, to support a new commission at the Royal Court.

PUBLIC FUNDING
Arts Council England, London
British Council
European Commission Representation in the UK

CHARITABLE DONATIONS
American Friends of the Royal Court
Martin Bowley Charitable Trust
Gerald Chapman Fund
City Bridge Trust
Cowley Charitable Trust
The H and G de Freitas Charitable Trust
The Dorset Foundation
The John Ellerman Foundation
The Eranda Foundation
Genesis Foundation
J Paul Getty Jnr Charitable Trust
The Golden Bottle Trust
The Haberdashers' Company
Paul Hamlyn Foundation
Jerwood Charitable Foundation
Marina Kleinwort Charitable Trust
The Leathersellers' Company
The Andrew Lloyd Webber Foundation
John Lyon's Charity
The Andrew W Mellon Foundation
The David & Elaine Potter Foundation
Rose Foundation
Royal Victoria Hall Foundation
The Dr Mortimer & Theresa Sackler Foundation
The Steel Charitable Trust
John Thaw Foundation
The Garfield Weston Foundation

CORPORATE SUPPORTERS & SPONSORS
BBC
Bloomberg
Coutts
Ecosse Films
Grey London
Kudos Film & Television
MAC
Moët & Chandon
Oakley Capital Limited
Sky Arts
Smythson of Bond Street
White Light Ltd

BUSINESS ASSOCIATES, MEMBERS & BENEFACTORS
Auerbach & Steele Opticians
Bank of America Merrill Lynch
Hugo Boss
Lazard
Louis Vuitton
Oberon Books
Peter Jones
Savills
Vanity Fair

DEVELOPMENT ADVOCATES
John Ayton MBE
Elizabeth Bandeen
Kinvara Balfour
Anthony Burton CBE
Piers Butler
Sindy Caplan
Sarah Chappatte
Cas Donald (Vice Chair)
Allie Esiri
Celeste Fenichel
Emma Marsh (Chair)
William Russell
Deborah Shaw Marquardt (Vice Chair)
Sian Westerman
Nick Wheeler
Daniel Winterfeldt

Supported by
**ARTS COUNCIL
ENGLAND**

young writers festival 2012

Debut plays from young British playwrights with original and diverse stories to tell.

30 – 31 March, 6pm, £8

reflection
festival reading

by **Rianna Mitchell-Henry**
director **Gbolahan Obisesan**

13 – 14 April, 6pm, £8

where the shot rabbits lay
festival reading

by **Brad Birch**
director **Nick Bagnall**

28 March, 10.15pm, Free

afterdark
spoken word in the cafe bar

Inua Ellams, Polarbear and **Kate Tempest**
(non-ticketed, entry first-come, first-served)

online playwriting toolkit

Inspiring tips and advice from Royal Court writers past and present. Read, watch and listen. Be inspired!
ywf.royalcourttheatre.com

coming next to jerwood theatre upstairs...

26 Apr – 26 May

belong

co-production with **Tiata Fahodzi**
by **Bola Agbaje**
director **Indhu Rubasingham**

Set in the political heat of London and Nigeria, this satirical new play calls into question our notion of home.
Tickets £20 / Mondays £10

020 7565 5000   www.royalcourttheatre.com

The Young Writers Festival is supported by the National Lottery through Arts Council England and is in partnership with the European Commission Representation in the UK, with additional support from the Dr. Mortimer and Theresa Sackler Foundation.

The Young Writers Festival Development Phase has been supported by John Lyon's Charity.

LOTTERY FUNDED

European Commission

JOHN LYON'S CHARITY

Principal Sponsor

Coutts

Supported by
ARTS COUNCIL ENGLAND

Vera Vera Vera

Acknowledgements

Thank you to the Royal Court family for taking a chance and giving *Vera* a life. Thank you to everyone who has worked to develop and produce the play. Your support has been invaluable. Thank you to Danny, Danielle, Tommy, Abby and Ted for everything they have done and are about to do. Thank you to Ben, Tom and Nic. Thank you to my friends who have been with *Vera* since day one.

The biggest thank you to my friend Jo McInnes for the love and life that she has given to *Vera*. Jo, forget about it mate.

This play is for my Mum, my Dad, my Brother and Francis with all of my love and gratitude. Without them I would probably be Emily.

There is no such thing as a soldier. I see death as a private event, the destruction of the universe in the brain and in the senses of one man, and I cannot see any man's death as a contributing factor in the success or failure of a military campaign.

— *The Resurrection of a Life*, William Saroyan, 1935

Characters

Charlie, *sixteen years old. Charlie is intelligent and bold. Sometimes her views on the world spill out without her being able to control it. She is Bobby's cousin.*

Sammy, *sixteen years old. Sammy is a boxer. He has been kicked out of most of his lessons at school and now only attends part time. Sammy has views on the world that seem to be of an 'old soul'.*

Emily, *twenty-four years old. Although Emily is tough and will fight anybody who offers it she is tired and longs for peace and quiet. She battles to keep up with Danny and fails to soften for Lee who she has been sleeping with secretly for a number of months. She is Danny and Bobby's sister.*

Danny, *twenty-six years old. Danny is violent in the way that he speaks to people and often violent through action. He takes and deals drugs. He is Emily's and Bobby's brother.*

Lee, *twenty-three years old. Lee is Bobby's oldest and best friend. He believes in working all week to play at the weekend. He has been sleeping with Emily secretly for a number of months.*

The play is set in the present, in Kent.

Notes on time: the events in Scenes One, Three and Five occur on the same day in April; those in Scenes Two and Four occur on the same day three months earlier, in January.

Scene One

Blackout. 'As Time Goes By' sung by Vera Lynn begins to play. The music continues as lights come up on **Charlie**.

She sits in her school uniform in her area away from the school at lunch time. She is waiting for **Sammy**. **Charlie** *has a packed lunch box and is eating some sandwiches. She is reading a copy of* Romeo and Juliet. *We see her alone for some time as the music fades.*

Sammy *enters in his school uniform. He throws his bag down next to her but doesn't look at her. Furious about something.*

Charlie   What's wrong with you?

Sammy   Nothing.

Charlie   Liar.

Sammy   I ain't.

Charlie   You are. Something's wrong because you just threw your bag down and you ain't even looked at me.

Sammy   Nothing's wrong.

Charlie   Look at me then.

He looks at her.

Charlie   What's the matter?

Sammy   Know that fucking prick Jamie Jones? Know him right? I'm going to fucking batter him mate.

Charlie   Why?

Sammy   Because he's a fucking prick.

Charlie   Yeah I know that but why?

Sammy   I don't know it's just his personality ain't it?

Charlie   You want to beat him up because of his personality?

Sammy   No his fucking personality is a prick.

Charlie   Oh right. So why do you want to beat him up?

Sammy   I've just told you Char.

Charlie   Yeah but I mean, like, he must of done something to you.

Sammy   Ain't done nothing to me mate, nothing that prick could do could bother me.

Charlie   But you said you were going to fucking batter him.

Sammy   I am. Right, I'm in fucking Sports Studies right? Playing football and he just takes me out, double boots me straight in the fucking shin! So I got up, right, and I went to him 'What did you do that for you fucking prick, you fucking wanker what you doing?' And he just laughs at me right?

Charlie   Yeah.

Sammy   Yeah just laughs in my face and goes to walk away so I pushed him and he turns round and gets right in my face and he's like 'Fuck's your problem bruv? Who you pushing bruv? Fuck do you think you're doing bruv?'

Charlie   Why's he keep calling you bruv?

Sammy   I don't know, right, so I go to him 'What you calling me bruv for? I ain't your fucking bruv mate, trust me, what the fuck's your problem Jamie?' 'I was going for the ball, calm down bruv' he goes to me.

Charlie   Why does he keep calling you bruv for?

Sammy   I don't know, talking to me like he's from London and that.

Charlie   Why's he doing that for?

Sammy   I don't know. But I let it go right, I think 'Sammy mate there ain't no point in stressing over this fucking prick so just let it go, you'll get yourself in trouble so just let it go right?'

Charlie   I'm glad that you did that.

Sammy   Yeah and then I'm in the changing room and him and all his fucking bent mates start winding me up.

Charlie   Saying what?

Beat.

Sammy   Just saying shit and that.

Charlie   What were they saying?

Sammy   It don't matter what they were saying, Char, just proper winding me up and that. So I fucking told Jamie Jones 'See you mate, meet me tonight and we'll have it out good and proper then'.

Charlie   What do you mean?

Sammy   I mean I'm meeting him tonight and I'm going to have it out with him good and proper.

Charlie   Yeah, what do you mean 'have it out good and proper'?

Sammy   He's been fucking winding me up for weeks Char, I've told him to leave it out but he won't so I'm going to meet him tonight, over the back of Scratchers Field, and I'm going to beat the fuck out of him.

Charlie   What, like, punch him in the face and that?

Sammy   Punch him fucking everywhere Char.

Charlie   Right.

Beat.

Sammy   What's the matter with you?

Charlie   Nothing.

Sammy   What's wrong?

Charlie   I think you should calm down, mate.

Sammy   I am calm mate, I'm chilled out babe it don't fuss me as long as Jamie Jones knows I'm going to batter him.

Charlie   Right.

Silence.

He sits next to her. He looks at her book on the ground.

Sammy   What's that for?

Charlie   *Romeo and Juliet.*

Sammy   Yeah I know what's it for?

Charlie   Coursework ain't it.

Sammy   Fuck that.

Charlie   You still got to do it.

Sammy   I don't do English do I?

Charlie   Just because you been kicked out you still got to do it.

Sammy   No I ain't.

Charlie   You won't even get a 'G'.

Sammy   Don't care I can read, write and talk can't I? I've seen the film anyway.

Charlie   I don't understand it.

Sammy   It's proper easy.

Charlie   I get confused with who's who.

Sammy   Do you want me to explain it?

Charlie   You don't know it.

Sammy   I do. Right, Romeo's from one family right? Juliet's from a different family, their two families fucking hate each other right? And anytime the cousins or the uncles or that see each other they have a fight and beat the fuck out of each other. Then they have a party and Romeo and Juliet have a bit of a dance and a bit of a kiss then they love each other and get married right? But then they all start shooting each other and she gets the hump and he gets kicked out the country and her dad's like, 'You're going to marry this fella who's proper rich and that right?' Then Juliet takes these drugs that make her look dead and Romeo's meant to come rescue her but then he actually thinks she is dead so then he tops himself and then she's like 'What am I meant to do now? Everything's all fucked up and that' so then she shoots herself right? So then they're both dead and everyone finds out and the two dads in the families make friends and that's it.

Charlie   Proper confusing that is mate.

Sammy   Watch the film and it's proper easy.

Charlie   I don't like it.

Sammy   Thought you hadn't seen it?

Charlie   No not the film, the story, all fighting and arguing with each other. Then they all die. And actually if someone had just gone 'hold on a minute actually we proper love each other' their dads could of just sorted it out then no one would of died.

Sammy   Then there wouldn't be a play though.

Charlie   Then I wouldn't have to do shitty coursework.

Sammy   Good point.

Beat.

Charlie   I'm scared about that now.

Sammy   About what?

Charlie   You fighting Jamie Jones.

Sammy   I knew you were going to say that.

Charlie   Sorry.

Sammy   Why you scared?

Charlie   Just because I am.

Sammy   Don't be.

Charlie   But I am now.

Sammy   Why though?

Charlie   In case someone gets hurt.

Sammy   Someone will get fucking hurt, Jamie Jones will, mate, trust me.

Charlie   That's what I mean.

Sammy   What's the problem with that then?

Charlie   I don't like it.

Sammy   You're scared in case he gets hurt?

Charlie   I'm scared in case anyone gets hurt.

Beat.

Sammy   You like him or what?

Charlie   What?

Sammy   You just said you were scared in case he gets hurt.

Charlie   In case anyone gets hurt.

Sammy   You're scared in case he gets hurt you said.

Charlie   Scared about you fighting.

Sammy   You like him or what?

Charlie   Fuck off.

She goes to pick up her lunch box and bag and leave.

Sammy   Charlie.

Charlie   Fuck off.

Sammy   I didn't mean it.

Charlie   You're a dickhead you are.

Sammy   I know.

Charlie   I don't like it when you fight.

Sammy   I know.

Charlie   Last time I saw you fight your nose bled down your chest.

Sammy   That was boxing.

Charlie   Same as fighting.

Sammy   It's not.

Charlie   You're a dickhead.

Sammy   I know. Put your lunch box down please.

She does.

He goes and sits next to her, kicks her book.

Sammy   Fucking *Romeo and Juliet*.

Charlie   I like the name Romeo.

Sammy   Do you?

Charlie   Yeah. How come's no one ever calls their kid anything like that no more?

Sammy   David Beckham did.

Charlie   Yeah but he can because he's proper famous so no one's going to tell him he's given his little boy a stupid name are they?

Sammy   I thought you said you like it.

Charlie   I do. I'd name my little boy Romeo. Or Horatio. Everyone has well boring names nowadays.

Sammy   I like my name. 'Sammy'.

Charlie   The name Sam reminds me of 'Spam'.

Sammy   'Spam'? What the pink ham stuff that comes in the tin?

Charlie   Yeah.

Sammy   Oh right.

Charlie   I like it though.

Sammy   Thanks.

Charlie   I don't like my name.

Sammy   You don't like Charlie?

Charlie   That's not my name though is it? My name's Charlene.

Sammy   That's fucking horrible that is.

Charlie   I know, I hate it.

Sammy   I like Charlie though that's proper nice. I like saying it and I like calling you it and that.

Beat.

Charlie   Can I come with you tonight?

Sammy   Where?

Charlie   When you go and fight Jamie.

Sammy   You won't like it.

Charlie   I have seen fights before you know.

Sammy   Yeah and you always cry.

Charlie   I won't this time.

Sammy   It ain't a good idea, Char. I'll get distracted worrying about you.

Charlie   I want to see that you don't get hurt.

Sammy   You don't need to be worrying.

Charlie   Please can I just come please?

Sammy   Don't cry though.

Charlie   I won't. Does that mean yes then?

Sammy   It's up to you.

Beat.

Sammy   What are you eating?

Charlie   The usual.

Sammy   Jam sandwiches?

Charlie   Yeah.

Sammy   What sort of jam?

Charlie   Strawberry.

Sammy   Nice.

Charlie   Do you want one?

Sammy   No thank you. Why do you always have jam?

Charlie   What else is there to have?

Sammy   Cheese?

Charlie   Cheese is dry.

Sammy   Ham?

Charlie   I don't like eating meat cold. It makes me think of how the animal died.

Sammy   That's a good reason to have jam then.

Charlie   Do you want a Penguin?

Sammy   No thank you.

Charlie   I put in an extra one for you so I think you should have it.

Sammy   Give me it then.

She gets the Penguin out of the lunch box and gives it to him.

Lights fade.

Scene Two

Blackout. 'Wish Me Luck as You Wave Me Goodbye' sung by Vera Lynn plays at the end of Scene One and through the transition into Scene Two. Lights up as music fades.

Maria's kitchen. **Emily** *and* **Danny** *sit at the kitchen table across from each other. There is a bottle of vodka on the table, three glasses and an ashtray. She is dressed in a tight black top, black jeans and* *black boots that have a heel on them. He has on a white shirt, a black skinny tie, waistcoat, black trousers and shoes. His black coat sits over the back of the chair.*

Emily *watches* **Danny** *as he reads something.*

Some time.

Emily   Do you think it's alright?

He doesn't look up and carries on reading.

Emily   No?

He carries on reading.

Emily   Do you think it's alright or not?

Danny   I ain't finished reading it, shut up.

He goes back to reading.

Emily   Fucking hell Dan, it's only about eight lines long.

Danny   Alright, I'm a slow reader shut up.

He carries on reading, she waits. He finishes and throws the bit of paper across the table to her.

Emily   It's alright ain't it?

Danny (*shrugs*)   Yeah.

Emily   What's wrong with it?

Danny   Nothing.

Emily   Why you saying it like that for then?

Danny   It's a load of shit.

Emily   What?

Danny   It's all lies.

Emily   How is it all lies?

Danny   You've lied.

Emily   No I ain't I've just said who he was and what he was.

Danny   No, you've told lies.

Emily   I ain't fucking lied Danny.

Danny   You have Em, he weren't like that was he? Unless me and you are talking about two different people? That is not what he was like so you've lied.

Emily   I ain't lied. You write it then if you've got something better to say.

Danny   I ain't writing fuck all Em, I ain't got fuck all to say about him.

Emily   You've got plenty to say now.

Danny   You asked me to read it.

Emily   Fuck knows why I bothered.

Danny   And after I read it I've decided it's all bollocks. Don't ask me if you don't want to know. Fuck knows why you're bothering anyway, nobody's going to turn up.

Emily   They are Dan.

Danny   They ain't Em.

Emily   The woman rung here in the week and told me they were sending someone.

Danny   They won't.

Emily   And she told me that she wanted to know what I was saying on behalf of the family and that I might have to do a piece to camera.

Danny   A piece to camera?

Emily   Yeah.

Danny   You're off your fucking head you are. Who's going to put you on telly?

Emily   I don't want to be on telly you prick, I'm just telling you what the woman said to me.

Danny   They won't send anyone. Why would they bother? People die every day, what makes him special that they would put it on the telly?

Lee *enters from the internal door. He is dressed in the same kind of clothes as* **Danny**.

Lee   She won't get up.

Emily   I told you that.

Lee   She won't even answer me, I'm talking to her and she ain't even blinking. There's fuck all going on.

Emily   I told you that, just leave her to it.

Lee   I thought she'd get up today, face on, fag on the go and braving it do you know what I mean? I can't believe no one's here.

Emily   She told me I had to tell them they weren't allowed.

Lee   Even your Aunty Linda?

Emily   Aunty Linda told her yesterday she had to get out of bed and sort herself out and mum told her to fuck off before she skinned her alive.

Lee   Fucking hell, that's a bit strong ain't it?

Emily   Best just to leave her to it.

Danny   Lee, Em thinks she's going to be on the telly.

Lee   Eh?

Danny   She thinks the news are coming to cover the funeral. She's been practising her speech and everything.

Emily   You're such a prick.

Lee   They rang in the week and said they were coming. Em's got to do a piece to camera.

Danny   Oh fuck me you two!

Emily   See?

Beat.

Danny   Read it to him then.

Emily   What?

Danny   Read it to him Em. Let Lee hear your piece to camera.

Emily   No.

Danny   Go on read it to him.

Emily   I don't want to read it to him.

Danny   I'm telling you to read it.

Emily   And I'm telling you no.

Danny   Right I'll read it to him.

Danny *grabs the piece of paper and stands up.*

Danny   'My brother was a charming and bright young man /

Emily   / Shut up Danny.

Danny   'who was brave and strong when others would be scared and frightened /

Emily   / Shut up.

Danny   'my family and I will miss him every day and nothing will ever replace /

Emily   Fuck off Danny!

He stops, looks at her and throws the piece of paper on the table.

Danny   Read it to him then.

Beat.

She picks up the paper and begins to read.

Emily   'My brother was a charming and bright young man who was brave and strong when others would be scared and frightened. My family and I will miss him every day and nothing will ever replace the hole that has been left by Bobby's death. I pray that those who knew him take comfort in the memories they have of him. Bobby was always full of life, would do anything for anyone and was always the bubbliest person in the room. He died serving his country and me and my family will always be proud of the man he was.'

Beat.

Lee   That's lovely Em.

Danny   You can't say he was bubbly, that makes him sound like a poof, only birds are bubbly ain't they?

Emily   No.

Danny   They are Em you're making him sound like a big gay. And that bit about doing anything for anyone, fucking hell.

Lee   That part is true Dan though ain't it? Bobby would give anything to anyone, give you his last pound if you needed it.

Danny   Yeah because he was soft as shit. And by the way I think it might be slightly inappropriate for you to say about him dying serving his country.

Emily   What you going on about?

Danny   Why highlight the one thing that he was completely shit at?

Emily   How was he shit at it?

Danny   Because he was shot in the face Em.

Emily   Fuck off Danny.

Danny   Have you got fake eyelashes on?

Emily   No.

Danny   Yes you have.

Emily   It's mascara you fucking knob.

Danny   And you've had your nails done.

Emily   I always have my nails done.

Danny   You're getting all dressed up because you think you're going to be on telly.

Emily   No I ain't.

Danny   You are.

Emily   Fuck off.

Danny   You're getting yourself all whored up in case there's some soldiers there ain't you?

Emily   You're a knob.

Danny   Like a soldier don't you Em?

Emily   Fuck off.

Danny   You want to fuck a solider don't you?

Emily   Yes Dan. That's what I'm doing, whoring myself up in case there's soldiers there that I can fuck at my brother's funeral.

Danny   Good girl.

Emily   Or I might see if the vicar wants a quick blow job before we start the service.

Danny   You've done worse.

Emily   Fuck you.

Danny   No Em. You can't fuck me. I'm your brother.

Emily   You're not my brother. I only had one brother and he was recently gunned down by Arabs.

Danny   Yeah and don't I know about it. I bet I wouldn't get all this fuss if I got shot.

Emily   Probably not. Go and get me a gun and we can find out.

Danny   Ain't I your brother then?

Emily   It's never been proven. Thank fuck.

Danny   I'm the head of this family.

Emily   You're the useless come that Dad left in Mum to haunt her.

Danny   Our dad's not dead.

Emily   I know. Shame ain't it?

Danny   Who am I if I'm not your brother?

Emily   Couldn't tell you Dan, I've been trying to work it out my whole life. I don't know where you came from or who you belong to but I do know that no one wants to claim you, no one wants you to belong to them.

Danny   I belong to you Em. I'm your drug dealer.

Emily   If you like.

Danny   You love me when I supply you with illegal substances.

Emily   I love everyone when you supply me with illegal substances you fucking idiot. It's called MDMA.

Danny   Dad told Mum to have you aborted.

Emily   Did he?

Danny   Yeah.

Emily   He was a clever cunt weren't he?

Danny   Full of bright ideas.

Emily   Please stop talking.

Danny   If he could see what you are now, the way you behave, he'd break your nose and jaw.

Emily   Would he Dan?

Danny   Yeah he would. He'd break your nose and your jaw to stop you sniffing coke and giving blow jobs. Maybe I'll do it.

Beat.

Danny   Lee, you must be the only one of Bobby's mates that's going to be there today who Em ain't fucked.

Emily   Shut up.

Lee   Is that right?

Danny   Oh yeah. She's had it with most of them.

Emily   Fuck off.

Danny   Didn't you know that Lee?

Lee   No.

Danny   Didn't you tell that to Lee, Emily?

Emily   Shut up.

Danny   Lost count of the number you've fucked by now ain't you Em?

Emily   Least they say yes to me. You don't know the meaning of the word 'no' do you Dan?

Danny   She didn't tell you Lee?

Lee   No she never mentioned it.

Danny   Oh yeah. You name them, she's fucked them. Since she was fifteen she's fucked every friend that Bobby brought through the front door.

Lee   I never knew that Dan.

Danny   That surprises me Lee. I thought you would have had a go yourself.

Lee   Not me mate.

Danny   Fair play son. All the rest of Bobby's mates have. Bobby would stand in the pub and they would all talk about how they'd done her, which way, where, what for. See, if that was me I'd batter every single one of them, mate, I wouldn't let no one talk about my sister like that. Even if what they were saying was true. But Bobby never opened his mouth. Because Bobby couldn't lie, he weren't capable of doing it was he? So he would just stand and listen when all of his mates talked about how they had fucked her. Like a pig being turned over on a spit roast. To do the other side.

Beat, **Danny** *watches* **Lee** *who looks straight back at him.*

Danny *breaks away raising his glass.*

Danny   Right then, Ladies and Gentleman, can you please raise your glasses to toast my little baby brother Bobby. May he rest in peace up with the angels.

He drinks. **Lee** *and* **Emily** *do the same.*

Lee   Is that all you've got to say on him then Dan?

Beat.

Danny   Eh?

Lee   What would you say about Bobby? If he weren't like how Em's written. What would you write?

Danny   I wouldn't write fuck all.

Lee   Why's that?

Danny   You being funny Lee?

Lee   No I'm just asking you what you'd say.

Danny   What would I say mate?

Lee   Yeah.

Danny   I'd say the truth son that's what I'd say.

Lee   Yeah? And what's that Dan?

Danny   I'd say what everyone knows mate. I'd say that my little brother Bobby was thick as shit. You could say jump to Bobby and he'd ask 'how high'. I'd say that the worst fucking thing that anyone could have done was let him go out to Arab land and give him a gun to defend himself with when he couldn't even hold his two fists up in front of his face. I'd say that if he felt like playing with guns I could have given him one and I would of taught him how to use it.

Lee And that would be the truth would it?

Danny Too right it would be son.

Lee Right.

Danny Is there a problem with that Lee?

Lee Nah.

Danny Looks like there is.

Lee Just think you must be talking about someone else Dan.

Danny Really?

Lee Yeah, mate. That ain't the Bobby I knew.

Danny Ain't it?

Lee Yeah I think you've got confused.

Danny Have I son?

Lee Yeah mate.

Danny I should know mate. Unless you think I'm a liar Lee?

Lee I'm not saying that.

Danny Well, you're obviously saying fucking something. You seem to have an answer for everything that's your problem Lee, son.

Emily Shut up Dan.

Danny What?

Emily Just shut up. Stop talking for fuck sake.

Danny Does everyone want to have a go at me today or what? 'Let's see who can have a row with Danny on the day he buries his brother' is it?

Emily Lee didn't mean nothing.

Danny Yes he did. He always does.

Emily   No he didn't.

Lee   No I didn't.

Danny   You get saucy Lee, that's your problem. You talk like you want to argue with everyone. Now it don't fuss me but I tell you what, son, word of warning and that, one day you'll say the wrong thing to someone and they'll smash a glass in your face and scar you for life.

Lee   Right.

Danny   Just to warn you. Some people are like that.

Beat.

Danny   Right, I'll see you in a bit.

Emily   Where you going?

Danny   I've got some people to see.

Emily   Who? The car's going to be here in a minute.

Danny   I'll take my car.

Emily   No, Dan. You're coming in the car with me and Lee.

Danny   I've got to go and drop some stuff off to someone.

Emily   What stuff?

Danny   Stuff.

Emily   You told me you didn't have any.

Danny   No I didn't. I said I didn't have any for you.

Emily   Who's it for then?

Danny   Leon.

Emily   Fuck off Dan. Why can't I have some?

Danny   I ain't got none for you.

Emily   You've got some for Leon.

Danny   He pays for his.

Emily   I'm your sister.

Danny   You're not my sister. It's never been proven remember?

Emily   I need it today, it'll stop me hurting.

Danny   Well, you're just going to have to suffer ain't you?

Beat.

I'll meet you there then. Oh and if when you arrive you see this sign on the door please don't be alarmed.

He pulls out a sign that reads 'No brown people allowed'.

Lee   What the fuck is that?

Danny   It's a sign to go on the front of the church.

Emily   No Danny.

Lee   Are you fucking mental?

Danny   No brown people allowed.

Emily   You ain't putting that up.

Danny   I fucking am.

Emily   You fucking ain't.

Danny   Who's going to stop me?

Emily   I fucking am.

Danny   No you won't. My brother was shot in the face by Arabs and Afghans and I don't want any brown people at his funeral. I don't think that's unreasonable.

Emily   It's unstable you prick.

Lee   James and his family are coming. Please don't put that up Danny, mate. That's going to really upset people, Bobby's mates, Danny please.

Danny   I went round there in the week and told them they weren't welcome.

Emily   You did what?

Danny   No brown people allowed.

Emily   He ain't an Arab, he's a black you knob!

Danny   No, Emily, he's brown. No brown people allowed.

Lee   We went to primary school with James. His mum looked after Bobby when he split his head open when he fell out the tree and your mum was at work. You can't do that Danny, that's not right, mate honestly it ain't.

Danny   No brown people allowed.

Lee   What's the matter with you?

Danny   You what?

Lee   What's wrong with you? It's a fucking funeral.

Danny   I know that.

Lee   Your nan and granddad are going to see that.

Danny   They ain't brown.

Lee   Why do you have to do this to people?

Danny   Do what?

Lee   You ain't putting that sign up.

Danny   You going to stop me then Lee? Eh? Are you son?

Lee   Danny, I tell you what, don't keep fucking call me son. I ain't your son. I ain't your mate and you ain't putting that fucking sign up.

Danny   My brother's funeral. My mum's drifting through space on Prozac and my sister too busy trying to find a soldier to fuck. Someone needs to take charge Lee.

Lee   He hated the fucking sight of you.

Beat.

Danny   What?

Lee   He hated you Danny. He thought you were a cunt, mate.

Danny   Did he?

Lee   Yeah.

Danny   Is that right?

Lee   Yeah it is yeah. And I'll tell you something else. If anyone shouldn't be allowed to go, it should be you. I watched you bully him his whole life and I watched you let your mates take the piss out of him. And the reason he thought you were a cunt is because you are a cunt, mate. And no one wants to see your face today. And no one wants you there. And if I was your mother I'd be laid up in bed out of my head on prescription drugs as well. Because your mother has been dealt a truly, traumatically shit hand. Bobby's dead and you're still breathing. Imagine how that makes your mother feel. That's a fucking walking talking tragedy that is.

Emily   Please shut up Lee.

Lee   Why Em? Why do I need to shut up?

Emily   Just please shut up.

Lee   No I won't. See, your brother was beautiful and I loved him with my whole heart. And you are an ugly cunt and you waste good air that Bobby could still be breathing.

Beat.

Danny   You finished.

Lee   Yeah.

Danny   Good. I'm going.

Danny *gets up and moves to the back door.*

Danny   When I've finished burying my brother I'm going to cut you open. I'm going to break a glass and slice your face open.

He leaves through the door.

Emily *and* **Lee** *look at each other.*

Lights fade.

Scene Three

Blackout. 'Faraway Places' sung by Vera Lynn plays at the end of Scene Two and throughout the transition into Scene Three change. Music fades as lights come up.

A park. **Charlie** *and* **Sammy** *sit on a bench, it's night time.* **Sammy** *drinks from a bottle of Stella and has another three on the floor by his foot in a Co-op bag.* **Charlie** *checks her phone, sends a text. She puts her phone away. Gets it back out, checks the time, then puts it back away again.*

Silence for some time.

Sammy   You ain't got to hang about.

Charlie   Eh?

Sammy   I said you ain't got to hang about, Char, if you got somewhere to be or someone to see or something like that then you ain't got to hang about. You can go or something if you want.

Charlie   Why you saying that?

Sammy   Just if you got somewhere to be or that then you can go.

Charlie   Why you saying that for?

Sammy   Keep checking your phone Char.

Charlie   Checking the time Sam.

Sammy   Checking the time every thirty seconds or something. You don't need to check it you could just ask me 'Sammy, what's the time?' and I'll tell you the time's thirty seconds since you last checked.

Charlie   Sorry, I just like to know what the time is.

Sammy   I'm a big boy I don't need you here if you got somewhere to be.

Charlie   Don't you want me here?

Sammy   I ain't bothered Char, it don't fuss me babe you asked if you could be here so I said yeah course and now fucking about with your phone every five minutes seems like you don't want to be.

Charlie   I'm a bit nervous to be honest Sammy.

Sammy   What you got to be nervous for?

Charlie   Case something happens.

Sammy   Case what happens, what's going to happen?

Charlie   I don't know.

Sammy   Then why you checking your phone for?

Charlie   I don't want you to be late.

Sammy   Eh?

Charlie   I don't want you to be late to meet him.

Sammy   Why you so worried about me being late for?

Charlie   I ain't worried I just don't want you to be late because you've told him when and where ain't you? And then if you ain't there on time and that he might start saying shit about you not being there and that.

Sammy   What if he does Char? The point is I am going to turn up and when I do I'm going batter the fuck out of him. To be honest I think me being late is the least of his worries.

Charlie   Alright.

Sammy   That's why I came here to have a few beers sort myself out sort my head and get myself ready for it and to be quiet.

She shuts up.

Sammy   'Charlie the talking clock'.

Charlie   Shut up.

Sammy   Do you want one of these? (*Offers the beer to her.*)

Charlie   No it's horrible, hate beer. Tastes like gone-off Weetabix.

Sammy   Gone-off Weetabix?

Charlie   Yeah.

Sammy   I've never had gone-off Weetabix.

Charlie   Nor have I actually but I reckon that's what they taste like.

Sammy   It's the hops.

Charlie   Ain't that the stuff vinegar's made out of?

Sammy   That's malt.

Charlie   Like the old biscuits?

Sammy   What old biscuits?

Charlie   Malt biscuits?

Sammy   Yeah. You don't want one then?

Charlie   No thanks.

He puts the empty bottle on the floor. Silence again.

Charlie   My nan used to buy malt biscuits.

Silence.

Charlie   You don't seem to want me here Sammy.

Sammy   Why are you saying that?

Charlie   You're really quiet and normally you talk to me loads.

Sammy   I'm just getting myself ready that's all. I like to be quiet before I fight.

Charlie   Is that what you do when you box and that?

Sammy   Yeah.

Charlie   Right. I didn't realise. Sorry.

Sammy   It's alright.

Charlie   So you don't talk before you fight then?

Sammy   I try not to. My uncle taught me that you've got to focus your energy and your mind and think about what it is you're about to do.

Charlie   So your uncle don't let you talk?

Sammy   It's part of the training. There are things you should and shouldn't do. It's about being fit and healthy and prepared and that.

Charlie   What else?

Sammy   I'm not allowed to drink.

Charlie   You're drinking now.

Sammy   Yeah but I'm not boxing now am I? I'm fighting.

Charlie   It's the same thing.

Sammy   No it's not. Boxing's a discipline. That's what my uncle told me first time I went to train, that it's a discipline not about going to kick someone's head in. It's about stamina and strength and self-control.

Charlie   You mean like being able to control yourself and that?

Sammy   Yeah. Like, I'm not allowed to wank.

Charlie   What?

Sammy   I'm not allowed to wank the week of a fight. My uncle reckons it's a test of self-control and resilience.

Charlie   Right. That's disgusting.

Sammy   Why is it?

Charlie   Why you talking to me about wanking for?

Sammy   I'm just telling you stuff.

Charlie   Why you telling me that?

Sammy   Because it helps you fight. You get an energy in you that comes from not doing it. It's frustration I think, not being able to release.

Charlie   Alright, I don't want to know the ins and outs of how you release yourself thanks Sam.

Sammy   I suppose a girl boxer would be told she couldn't wank before a fight either.

Charlie   Fucking hell Sam!

Sammy   What?

Charlie   Why you telling me that for?

Sammy   I don't know, I thought you wanted to know.

Charlie   I don't want to know about you wanking.

Sammy   I'm telling you that I don't wank.

Charlie   Either way I don't want to know, you're disgusting.

Sammy   How am I disgusting? Girls do it too.

She doesn't reply.

Sammy   Don't they?

Charlie   What you asking me for?

Sammy   Because you're a girl.

Charlie   So?

Sammy   Why you going red for?

Charlie   I'm not!

Sammy   Why you shouting?

Charlie   I'm not.

Sammy   It's only wanking.

Charlie   Fucking hell.

Sammy   Do you do it?

Charlie   Fuck off.

Sammy   I'm only asking.

Charlie   You're an idiot.

Sammy   You ain't got to be embarrassed.

Charlie   I ain't embarrassed mate, trust me, I think you're a fucking knob though.

Sammy   Why?

Charlie   Because you're disgusting.

Sammy   Look at me.

She doesn't.

Sammy   Char . . . Look at me.

She does.

They both laugh.

Sammy   I knew it!

Charlie   Fuck off you dickhead.

Sammy   I knew it Char!

Charlie   You're a wanker you are.

Sammy   So are you!

Charlie   Fuck off.

Sammy   You ain't got to be embarrassed.

Charlie   I'm not embarrassed, what have I got to be embarrassed about?

Sammy   About wanking, Char, it's only wanking mate.

Charlie   Don't bother me mate.

Sammy   You do it and you're embarrassed that I know.

Charlie   Fuck off.

Sammy   Don't you ever be embarrassed in front of me Char, I think you're gorgeous you know that. And you'd be even more gorgeous wanking I reckon.

Charlie   Fuck off Sam!

Sammy   Why do girls get embarrassed? They let boys do it to them so they must like doing it to themselves. Would you want a boy to finger you?

It's only a question.

She doesn't answer.

Sammy   Answer the question Char. It's only fingering.

She doesn't look at him or answer him.

Charlie   What about kissing.

Sammy   What?

Charlie   You don't ever ask me about kissing Sammy.

He can't look at her now. He stays looking forward throughout the next exchange.

Sammy   I wouldn't ask about kissing.

Charlie   Why not?

Sammy   Because I would just kiss you. I wouldn't ask if I could. I just would.

Charlie   Why do you have to ask me about fingering? It should be kissing first.

Sammy   I know!

Charlie   But you haven't asked if you can kiss me.

Sammy   I want you.

Charlie   You want me?

Sammy   I mean I want to kiss you.

Charlie   Why ain't you then?

Sammy   I don't know.

She moves herself so that her face is next to his, he still can't look at her.

Charlie   Kiss me if you want to.

He doesn't move.

Charlie   Go on then.

Pause.

Sammy   I can't. I don't want to lose my focus.

She stays close to his face for a moment and then moves away from him.

He moves to open another bottle of beer, drinks.

Sammy   You'd like my Uncle Steve.

Charlie   Do you think?

Sammy   Yeah, you'd love him. He's quality. Proper old-fashioned man he is. Boxed for years, deadly he was as well. I've told him about you he wants to meet you.

Charlie   I've met him. At the fight.

Sammy   Yeah but you only said 'Hello' and that was it. He wants to meet you proper.

Charlie   Right.

Sammy   He used to fight in the fields when he first started, used to fight the pikeys for money then he trained properly and won every match. Champion of Kent he was once. Proper proud of that. He don't do it no more, he's got a brick laying business.

Charlie   Yeah I remember you saying.

Sammy   He's fucking quality, mate. I love him. You'll love him.

Charlie   Will I?

Sammy   Yeah. Proper good he is. Love him to bits.

Silence.

Sammy   He knows your Aunty Maria.

Charlie   Does he?

Sammy   Yeah, apparently he used to take her out when they were younger.

Charlie   Right.

Sammy   Yeah, apparently Steve kept trying to get off with her and Aunty Maria weren't having none of it so she told him to do one.

Charlie   Yeah that sounds about right.

Sammy   That's mental that is ain't it?

Charlie   Yeah.

Sammy   Steve said she was mad when she was younger liked to have a good drink and dance and that.

Charlie   Yeah she did.

Pause.

Sammy   Steve said you look like her. He said it was like looking at Maria when she was sixteen. Do you think you look like her?

Charlie   Some people reckon I do.

Silence.

Sammy   That's Bobby's mum ain't it?

Charlie   Yeah.

Beat.

Sammy   How is she?

Charlie   She's alright.

Sammy   Has she gone back to work?

Charlie   Not yet.

Sammy   Is she going to?

Charlie   Don't know.

Sammy   Have you asked her?

Charlie   No.

Sammy   Has your mum asked her?

Charlie   Yeah. She don't argue with her though.

Sammy   Must be fucking horrible.

She nods.

Sammy   Does she go out?

Charlie   Course she goes out she's not disabled. She goes and does her shopping when she needs to and her and my mum go bingo on Wednesdays and Sundays.

Sammy   They go bingo?

Charlie   Yeah.

Sammy   Why?

She shrugs.

Beat.

Sammy   I don't know what I'd do if it was me.

Charlie   If what was you?

Sammy   If I was your Aunty Maria.

Charlie   Well, that would be fucking weird wouldn't it Sammy?

Sammy   What?

Charlie   If you were my Aunty Maria. That's too confusing to think about that is Sam it makes my brain hurt a bit actually.

Sammy   You know what I mean.

Charlie   Yeah.

Sammy   You don't ever talk about it Char.

Charlie   I know.

Sammy   You don't ever talk to anyone no more do you?

Charlie   I'm scared to open my mouth Sam.

Sammy   Why?

Charlie   Because I don't know what's going to come out of it.

Beat.

Sammy   I don't know what I'd do. If that had happened to me. I don't know how people survive it. I don't know how people get over it and carry on breathing and getting up and going out and that. Remember when Jack Edwards' mum died in Year 8? That was fucking horrible that was when he just kept bursting into tears in the middle of class for no reason.

Charlie   Well, it weren't for no reason was it? He was crying because his mum was dead.

Sammy   Yeah I know but you know what I mean. Bursting into tears like he just couldn't control it, he couldn't stop himself doing it. I don't think I'd be able to survive something like that, I'm not strong enough I would just feel too sad all the time, I'd be no good to no one.

Charlie   It's a fucking good job it's never happened to you then ain't it?

Sammy   Yeah. I suppose it is.

Silence. His phone goes off, he takes it out and reads a text.

Sammy   Time to go.

She doesn't move.

Sammy   Maybe you should wait here Char.

Charlie   Why?

Sammy   This might scare you.

Charlie   I'll be scared if you leave me here on my own. I don't like the dark.

He hides the carrier bag with beers in under the bench.

She gets up and they go.

Lights fade.

Scene Four

Blackout. 'When I Grow Too Old to Dream' sung by Vera Lynn plays at the end of Scene Three and throughout the transition into Scene Four. Lights raise as music fades. **Lee** *is alone in the kitchen. He has a bottle of vodka and two glasses on the table. It is night time.*

Emily *enters from the side door.*

Lee   She asleep?

Emily   Yeah.

Lee   Drink?

Emily   Yeah.

Emily *sits at the top of the table,* **Lee** *sits on the chair to the left of her. He pours them each a glass of vodka.*

They drink and smoke throughout.

Lee   You tired?

Emily   Fucked.

She pulls off her fake eyelashes.

Lee   They were fake?

Emily   Course they were fake. They were Cheryl Cole's.

Lee   Cheryl Cole's?

Emily   Yeah got them from Superdrug, cost me a fiver.

Lee   Why did you bother?

Emily   I thought I was going to be on telly didn't I? Got my nails done too.

He doesn't reply.

Emily   Do you want me to do you a sandwich?

Lee   I'm alright.

Silence.

Lee   You tired?

Emily   You asked me that.

Lee   Oh right. What did you say?

Emily   I told you I was fucked.

Silence. They drink and smoke.

Lee   Lots of people there weren't there?

Emily   I didn't invite them.

Lee   Someone put it on Facebook.

Emily   What?

Lee   The details of the funeral. It was done as an event. Said everyone was welcome.

Emily   A fucking Facebook event?

Lee   Yeah.

Emily   Cunts.

Lee   All your family were there at least.

Emily   Yeah.

Lee   Except for your mum.

Emily   Yeah.

Lee   Your Aunty Linda's girl, Charlie?

Emily   Yeah.

Lee   She really cried.

Emily   I know.

Lee   Horrible that was.

Emily She thought he walked on water that's why. Used to tell everyone about him.

Lee Right.

Emily I didn't tell anyone about him.

Lee Eh?

Emily I didn't tell anyone about him. I didn't tell anyone what he did.

Lee Why?

Emily Because I didn't know anything about it Lee, I couldn't even tell you where he was when he died, I couldn't tell you who the person was that did it to him or what they were a part of or why they had the hump and was fighting in the first place. I don't know fuck all about it.

Lee Me either.

Emily Lazy that is.

Lee No it ain't.

Emily Course it is.

Lee I don't think so. I didn't even ask him about it when he told me. I just said to him 'Think of the birds you'll get mate'.

Emily Of course you did.

Lee What does that mean?

Emily Nothing.

Lee What did it mean?

Emily Didn't mean nothing.

Lee Meant something.

Emily Just meant course you told him that. Course you told him 'Think of the birds you'll get'.

Lee   What's wrong with that?

Emily   Talking to him about girls.

Lee   Yeah, so? Me talking to him about girls what's the problem? Me and him used to always talk about girls.

Emily   What girls?

Lee   All girls.

Emily   But what girls?

Lee   Girls who we'd been with, girls who we wanted to be with.

Emily   All of them? You used to talk about all of them did you?

Lee   No not all of them.

Emily   You just said you talked to him about all the girls you'd been with or wanted to be with.

Lee   Not all of them though obviously.

Emily   Why not?

Lee   Why not what?

Emily   Why not all of them? What girls didn't you talk to him about?

Lee   Just different girls.

Emily   What ones?

Lee   All different ones.

Emily   Why didn't you tell him about every girl you'd been with?

Lee   Because I couldn't could I?

Emily   Why not? What makes some girls different to other ones, why didn't you tell him about all the girls?

Lee   Because I couldn't tell him I wanted to fuck his sister could I?

Beat.

Lee   And when I did fuck his sister I couldn't tell him about it.

Emily   Why?

Lee   Because he was my best friend.

Beat.

Emily   Do you feel guilty about it?

Lee   I do now. Yeah.

Emily   I don't. Even now he's died I don't.

Beat.

Lee   Maybe you should go to bed.

Emily   What?

Lee   Do you want to go to bed?

Emily   With you?

Lee   No, Em.

Emily   I thought you were offering.

Lee   Emily.

Emily   Lee.

Lee   Let it go.

Emily   I thought you were offering.

Lee   Don't.

Emily   I thought you were asking if you could take me to bed?

Lee   Just stop it.

Emily   Do you want to take me to bed?

Lee   Fucking stop it Em!

Emily   What? You bought it up. You said bed, I didn't say nothing about bed you were the one who started about us going to bed.

Lee   No, alright, I wasn't saying why don't we go to bed. I asked you if you were tired and you told me you were so I meant why don't you go to bed. Go to bed and go to sleep is what I meant.

Emily   I know what you meant Lee.

Beat.

Emily   Danny'll be home soon.

Lee   Don't talk to me about Danny.

Emily   Why? You scared?

Lee   I'm not scared of Danny.

Emily   You should be.

Lee   Well I ain't.

Emily   He'd cut you.

Lee   No he wouldn't.

Emily   If he found you here.

Lee   No he wouldn't Em.

Emily   In bed with me.

Lee   Fucking hell.

Emily   He'd cut you.

Lee   No he wouldn't Em. He wouldn't do fuck all. He didn't put that sign up did he?

Emily   You think you're better than him.

Lee   I think a piece of shit on the bottom of my shoe is better than him.

Emily   You two ain't that different.

Lee   Why do you defend him?

Emily   I don't defend him but I think you need to remember whose house you're sitting in and watch what you're saying.

Lee   Is it because you're scared of him?

Emily   I'm not scared of him.

Lee   You're shit scared of him.

Emily   No I'm not.

Lee   You are. That's why you talk like you do and act like you do.

Emily   Is it?

Lee   Yeah. You talk like something disgusting and you talk about fucking people and you talk about drugs. You asked him for sniff.

Emily   So?

Lee   It was your Bobby's funeral Em. Why did you ask him for sniff?

Emily   So that I could sniff it.

Lee   That's all because of him. That's not what you do. That's not what you're about.

Emily   Ain't it?

Lee   No.

Beat.

Lee   I don't like your voice when you talk to him. I don't like the words you use.

Emily   I couldn't give a fuck.

Lee   Yes you could.

Emily   No.

Lee   Yes you could, Em, you could give a fuck. You don't want me to be disgusted by you.

Emily   Why don't I? Who are you to me?

Lee   I saw your face when he said what he said this morning.

Emily   When he said what?

Lee   When he said . . . When he said that thing to me about you and Bobby's mates. You looked like you'd just had your ribs stamped on.

She doesn't look at him or answer him.

Lee   Have you slept with all of Bobby's mates?

Emily   I've slept with lots of people.

Lee   Was he lying Em?

She doesn't answer.

Lee   Did he say it just to do me over Em?

She doesn't answer.

Lee   Em, did Danny say that just to cut me? Is it true? Or was he lying Em?

Emily   Are you Bobby's friend?

Lee   Is that a yes?

Emily   Are you Bobby's friend Lee?

Lee   Is that a yes?

Emily   Were you his mate?

Lee   Is that a fucking yes?!

Emily   You were his best fucking friend weren't you?

He doesn't answer her.

Emily   Tell the truth and stop telling lies Lee. I fucked you and I'm his sister. You fucked me and you were Bobby's best friend. That's not a lie. That's the truth ain't it?

He doesn't answer.

Emily   On Bobby's eighteenth birthday when you all went to Cardiff for the weekend what was your present to him?

Lee   I don't remember.

Emily   Yes you do.

Lee   It was four years ago Em, I don't remember that far back.

Emily   Don't fucking lie to me Lee, you sit there and swear to me you don't remember.

Lee (*hushed*)   Keep your voice down.

Emily   Swear that you don't.

He doesn't reply.

Emily   What was it?

Lee   Sniff.

Emily   What?

Lee   Sniff.

Emily   Yeah, sniff. See, it's all truth. You were the one who gave Bobby his first go on sniff, not Danny. Danny told him he'd break his nose if he found him anywhere near it. It's all the truth Lee. Danny is a cunt but at least he's truthful about it.

He doesn't reply which causes the following to spill out of her.

We aren't good people Lee, we're shit. I am and so are you and so is everyone we know. We take drugs, we deal drugs, we steal things, we don't work. You can't make us all into saints because it was Bobby's funeral. You still fucked his sister and you still took pills with him every weekend. You can't make him into a hero because he was shot by Arabs because look at us. Yes he was beautiful, he had the sweetest heart but he was thick, he was fucking stupid, he didn't have an education because he didn't behave at school. He was too busy setting fire to things and all Mum and Dad ever did was tell him to stop being a little bastard and behave. And that's

why she's up there now. And why she couldn't get up today
and come and tell everyone about her little boy. Because she
fucking knows the truth. She knows what she's done and
what she's made.

You've spent the whole day trying to be polite and respectful
and telling everyone that he died for his country but that
isn't good because we are his country. I loved him and my
heart's broken now that he's dead but we are still shit. You
can't point Danny out to be the Devil standing alone. We still
do bad things. Our lives are bad. The least you could do is be
truthful about it.

Beat. He doesn't answer her.

Emily   I don't mean to upset you. All of us are suffering
and trying to work it out.

Lee   Yeah.

Emily   Can you pour me another drink please?

*She slides the glass in front of him. He pours her a drink and one for
himself.*

Lee   I suppose me and Danny are going to have to have it
out at some point about what I said to him this morning.

Emily   He is bigger than you ain't he?

Lee   A little bit.

Emily   He'll be face down on a bar somewhere by now.

Beat.

I heard him crying to Bobby that last weekend he was home.
They'd been out on the piss and Bobby had brought Danny
home and was trying to get him up the stairs and I think
Dan must of been sniffed up and that and he cried really
bad. I could hear him grabbing hold of Bobby and crying
at him not to go away. Bobby just kept telling him to 'sshh'
and I could hear him kissing Danny on the head and that
trying to calm him down. That's the only time I remember
Danny crying.

Lee   Bobby always cried.

Emily   Constantly. Anytime he was upset.

Lee   I've never known a boy to cry the way he did. Once when Danny was nine and me and Bobby were five he took us to the park. Danny was the first one to stand up on the swing, the other boys dared him to do it so course he did. And he fell off. Proper smacked his head onto the floor it made a really horrible noise. When he stood up his eyes were all watery. I thought he was going to cry, I was convinced of it, I don't know how he didn't. I remember he had a massive lump over his eye and Bobby was really panicked and that and he said to him 'Danny, do you want me to go and get Mum so she can put a bag of peas on it'. And he pulled Bobby's hair really hard so that Bobby fell on the floor and started crying and when Bobby asked him 'Why did you do that for Danny?' Danny came right up to him and grabbed the back of his head and dug his thumb into Bobby's eye until he fell on the floor again. Bobby cried his eyes out all the way home and when we got back here Danny told your mum that Bobby had tried standing up on the swing and had fallen off and that's why his eye was black. Me and Bobby never told your mum the truth. Fucking hell he did cry that day Em. I had to keep cuddling him to shut him up.

Beat.

Emily   No one gave anyone cuddles at the funeral did you notice that? Even my granddad just held my nan's hand but he didn't put his arm around her. No one gave anyone cuddles or kisses. It was like no one dared to touch each other.

Lee   I noticed it. I did give your nan a kiss when they left the pub though.

Emily   Of course you did. Bobby used to kiss and cuddle me all the time. He used to give me the best cuddles.

Lee   He used to give me the best kisses.

She laughs.

Emily   Yeah there was always something a bit strange about how long you two used to spend locked in his bedroom together.

Lee   We were usually smoking a joint.

Beat.

Emily   I cuddled my cousin Charlie in the toilets. She grabbed hold of me, crying, and kept saying the word 'dead' in my ear because she couldn't get her other words out. First time I've heard her speak since it happened. She just stopped talking completely. I held on to her and held her head still and said into her ear 'not dead, died. Bobby's not dead, he's just died'. 'Died' is peaceful. Calm.

Lee   That's better that is.

Emily   Bobby got the good heart didn't he?

Lee   The best.

Emily   Bobby got the good heart and Danny got the bad one.

Lee   Yeah.

Emily   Where do you think that leaves me?

Lee   What do you mean?

Emily   Bobby was good, Danny's bad. What does that make me?

Lee   You're good.

Emily   I'm not good like Bobby was though am I?

Lee   You're not bad like Danny is Em.

Emily   Ain't I?

Lee   No. As much as you try to be, you could never be as bad as him. People either have that in them or they don't and you just don't.

Emily   So what am I then? What does that make me? Good heart or bad heart?

Lee   –

Emily   Exactly. You can't tell me can you? My Bobby was so good. And I don't even know what my heart is.

He moves close to her but he doesn't touch her or answer her. She doesn't meet his look.

Emily   Are you staying with me tonight?

Lee   Yeah I was going to. Do you want me to?

Emily   Yes please.

They stay where they are.

Lights fade.

Scene Five

Blackout. 'From the Time You Say Goodbye' sung by Vera Lynn plays at the end of Scene Four and throughout the transition into Scene Five. Lights up and music fades.

Charlie *and* **Sammy** *enter, puffed out, adrenaline pumping.* **Sammy** *has just had the fight with Jamie Jones.*

Charlie   Fucking hell.

Sammy   Yeah.

Charlie   Mate, fucking hell.

Sammy *laughs. He goes back to the bench, pulls out the Co-op bag that he has hidden, takes out a bottle of Stella, takes out his lighter, pops the cap off and drinks rapidly.* **Char** *doesn't sit, she is unable to because of the urgency in her.*

Sammy   Sit down Char.

She moves to sit next to him on the bench.

He watches her then passes her the bottle, she drinks the whole bottle of Stella in one go.

Charlie   I think I'm going to be sick.

Sammy   I don't think they expected you to turn up.

They laugh.

Sammy   I don't think they expected you to be throwing punches.

They laugh. She begins to cry.

Sammy   Oi, what you doing? Why you crying? Don't get upset, I told you in the first place you shouldn't come. Didn't I? I did though didn't I?

Charlie   Yeah and what would you have done if I hadn't been there?

Sammy   What?

Charlie   They were all on you Sammy.

Sammy   No they weren't.

Charlie   They were Sammy.

Sammy   Who was all on me? I don't know what you're talking about. No one was fucking all on me.

Charlie   Sammy, I was holding you up and there were two this side and two this side punching you in the head.

Sammy   Yeah and I was punching them right back weren't I?

Charlie   Yeah but there was four of them.

Sammy   I was punching them back weren't I? Don't act like I didn't sort it out because you know I fucking did.

Charlie   I was scared.

Sammy   Why though?

Charlie   All I could think was if they got you on the floor they would kick you in the head. That's why I held on to you and tried to get round you and hold your head up so that they didn't get you on the floor.

Sammy   Yeah and they didn't get me on the floor did they? I had fucking Jamie Jones on the floor didn't I? Please don't get upset Char. Look at me, I'm fine, alright? I'm here, you're here and we are fine and we're laughing Char ain't we? Now wipe your tears because your snot's going everywhere.

She laughs, wipes her face with her sleeve to sort herself out.

Sammy   You got one fucking deadly punch on you Char, I wouldn't fight you.

Charlie   I'd knock you out mate.

Sammy   Yeah you would.

Beat.

Charlie   Makes me feel sick, fighting.

Sammy   Does it?

Charlie   Yeah proper.

Sammy   I'm sorry.

Charlie   It's alright. It's weird ain't it? You know like when someone pisses you off and in your head you think about having a fight with them and proper battering them like and in your head it's all smooth and that and you give them a proper beating. It's never like that though is it, it's messy and unclean.

Sammy   Its adrenaline.

Charlie   I don't like the sound of my voice in a fight. It sounds like the first time I ever heard myself scream. Does it make you feel sick?

Sammy   No.

Charlie   Does it make you feel like you're something special, hard and that?

Sammy   No course not.

Charlie   Do you not feel sick punching someone's face?

Sammy   I black out Char. I don't know what I've done until I come out of it and people tell me.

Charlie   Why did you fight Jamie?

Sammy   Because he's a prick.

Charlie   Yeah I know he's a prick and that but what did he do for you to fight him?

Sammy   It don't matter now.

Charlie   What does that mean?

Sammy   It don't matter.

Charlie   It does. Obviously it does. You just fucking broke the boy's nose you must have done it for a reason.

Sammy   I didn't break his nose.

Charlie   I think you did. I heard it. Why won't you tell me?

Sammy   Because you'll start crying again.

Charlie   Why will I?

Sammy   Because you will and I don't like it when you cry.

Charlie   Why will I cry?

Sammy   Because it's about you.

Charlie   What?

Sammy   He said something about you, Char, and I ain't going to tell you because you'll start crying again and I don't like it when you cry.

Charlie   I won't cry.

Sammy   You will.

Charlie   I fucking won't Sammy can you just tell me please? You can't say that and then not tell me.

Sammy   Alright, but don't start crying to me about it. He said . . . He told everyone . . .

Pause.

Charlie What?

Sammy Right, he told everyone he fingered you at Chelsea's house party.

Charlie He what?

Sammy He told all the boys that he fingered you at Chelsea's house party. He said that you were dancing with him to that Rihanna song and you were like proper grinding on him and that and then he put his hand up your skirt to start fingering you and you didn't stop him and you loved it and that.

Charlie Are you fucking joking?

Sammy No.

Charlie Is that actually what he said?

Sammy Yes Char that is what he actually said.

Charlie Are you fucking lying or what?

Sammy No Char I'm not that's what he told everyone alright?

Charlie What fucking Rihanna song?

Sammy I don't know he just said a Rihanna song I didn't ask the details.

Charlie Well he's fucking lying!

Sammy Alright.

Charlie I've never danced with Jamie Jones in my life! I hate him and I don't even like any new Rihanna songs so why would I be dancing with him in the first place?

Sammy I don't know, don't worry about it.

Charlie Well, it ain't fucking true. He never did that to me, I never danced with him I wouldn't even let him come near me. I don't even talk to him the prick.

Sammy Alright.

Charlie   When did he say this was supposed to of happened?

Sammy   At Chelsea's house party.

Charlie   What a fucking liar! I spent all night texting you anyway because you weren't there and then I went home didn't I? Remember we were texting all night?

Sammy   Yeah. I know, don't worry about it.

Charlie   How can I not worry about it? He's going round telling everyone shit like that everyone's going to think I'm a right slut.

Sammy   No they ain't.

Charlie   Obviously they are and I'm not even like that am I?

Sammy   I know you ain't Char.

Charlie   Yeah but I don't want you thinking that of me.

Sammy   I don't.

Charlie   Watch when I see him again I'm going to kick his fucking head in the lying little prick.

Sammy   Bit late now. That's what the fight was over. That's why I had the fight with him because I told him I weren't having him going round lying about you like that and I told him I was going to kick his fucking head in.

Silence.

Charlie   Thank you.

Sammy   You ain't got to thank me. I ain't having no one say shit like that about you. I hate it when they even say your name.

Charlie   Who?

Sammy   Boys.

Charlie   What boys?

Sammy   Every boy.

Beat.

Charlie   As long as you do know that it's a lie.

Sammy   I do.

Charlie   Good.

Pause.

Charlie   Because I wouldn't even be with anyone else.

Sammy   What do you mean?

Charlie   You know what I mean.

Sammy   Anyone else but who?

Charlie   You.

Sammy   Are you with me then?

Charlie   I don't know, am I? I was on your side in the fight. I was screaming for you.

Sammy   What?

Charlie   I was screaming your name in the fight, I didn't realise I was doing it until after.

Sammy   Screaming my name was ya?

Charlie   Yeah.

Sammy   Screaming it hard and loud was ya?

Charlie   Fuck off.

Sammy   Did it feel good screaming my name Char?

Charlie   Yeah it did Sammy.

Sammy   Did you love it?

Charlie   Yeah, I was wetting my pants while I was doing it.

Sammy   You ain't even given me a kiss to say thank you.

Charlie   You want me to kiss you?

Sammy   I think it would be nice of you.

Charlie   I tried to kiss you earlier and you shit yourself, wouldn't even look at me.

Sammy   I had to focus Char.

Charlie   You're a liar.

Sammy   How could I kiss you and then go and beat someone up? I wouldn't be able to concentrate properly and I would of lost.

Charlie   You missed your chance.

Sammy   Come here.

Charlie   What?

Sammy   Come over here and I'll kiss you then.

Charlie   Alright.

She doesn't move.

Sammy   Come here then, I dare you.

She moves to him. He takes her face in his hands and then kisses her. A moment. They break away from each other, she shifts to the other side of the bench and he moves to open his last beer and drinks.

Silence.

Sammy   Char?

Charlie   Yeah?

Sammy   I do know why you don't like fighting you know?

Charlie   Ok.

Pause.

Sammy   Is that why?

Charlie   Is what why?

Sammy   Your cousin?

Charlie   Yeah.

Sammy   I'm sorry for doing something that makes you feel like that, sick and sad. I proper hate it when you cry.

Charlie   I asked to come.

Sammy   I'm still sorry.

Silence.

Charlie   I know you want to ask me about it.

Sammy   What?

Charlie   About Bobby.

Sammy   I don't want to ask you about it.

Pause.

I just want you to know that I know that's why you're sad. I know that it's why you are like you are.

Charlie   Like what?

Sammy   Always on your own. Why you say weird shit sometimes.

Charlie   I don't tell lies.

Sammy   I didn't mean lies.

Pause.

I don't talk to anyone as much as you. In one day I say more words to you than anyone else.

Charlie   You have 97 per cent of my words in a day.

Sammy   That's a lot. You can say any words to me that you want.

Charlie   Ok.

Sammy   I'm not saying you've got to tell me what happened.

Charlie   I don't know what happened. I wasn't there.

Sammy   I don't mean what happened when it actually happened. I mean what happened when it happened to you.

Charlie I don't really know what happened when it happened to me. I stopped talking to everyone for about two weeks. More like a month actually.

Sammy Tell me to shut up and fuck off if I'm upsetting you.

Charlie You're not.

Sammy I don't want you to cry again.

Charlie I won't.

Sammy I read about it in the paper and that, that him and his mate was trying to help their other mate and they got caught up in it and that.

Charlie Yeah. I memorised what it said in the paper.

Sammy You memorised it?

Charlie Yeah, because people kept asking me about it so I just always told them what the paper said.

Sammy What did the paper say?

Pause. She looks at him and then begins.

Charlie He was killed on patrol in the Helmand province of south west Afghanistan. Bobby and his friend David were shot trying to save their mate Chris who had been shot in the leg and the stomach. David and Bobby were both killed and Chris survived. That's what I tell everyone when they ask. I memorised it so I had the facts because I don't know what happened to him.

His mum was at our house when the man came to tell her. We were sat there having our dinner, sausages I think, and my cousin Emily came through the door with this man. Soon as my aunty saw him she just started screaming and wailing like her throat was about to explode. She made a noise that I didn't know it was possible for humans to make. My mum grabbed hold of Em and both of them just fell on the floor and was crying and that. I didn't know what the fuck was going on, the man hadn't even opened his mouth. And then he said it. He was meant to be telling my aunty but he looked right at me, like I was the only one who could hear his words, like it was just us two left in the room and the rest of them had gone somewhere else. You know my dog Jerry? He threw up in the corner of the living room. I think he was scared from the noise my aunty had made. I got up and got some tissue to clear the dogs sick up because I didn't want it to stain the carpet and then I scrubbed it with Vanish. Then I was sick. I tried to stop myself by putting my hand over my mouth but it came out anyway and dripped through my fingers and on to the carpet. I don't know if it left a stain.

I don't really remember his funeral. My mum had people back to ours after the wake for a piss-up because my Aunty Maria wouldn't let anyone in her house. She didn't even go to the funeral. Mum said it was her responsibility. She made me go next door to my neighbour Lauren's house for 'a nice cup of tea and a bit of peace and quiet'. I didn't want to go, she knows I think Lauren's a fucking idiot. I go into her front room and her baby's crying in her shitty little Moses basket in the corner and I'm sitting on the sofa watching Lauren's boyfriend and his mate play *Call of Duty* on the Xbox. Can you believe how rude that is? Fucking *Call of Duty* where you pretend to be a soldier in the war and you see how many people you can kill and you go on loads of different missions, and use loads of different knives and guns and bombs and you stab people and shoot people and blow people up. On the Xbox. It made me so mad. I wanted to pull the fucking controllers out of their hands and smash their skulls in until their ears bled. I wanted to punch Lauren in the face, Sam, I wanted to hurt them really so much. Her boyfriend don't do nothing apart from smoke weed all day and play the Xbox, he's all skinny and that and he's always got a scab round his mouth. And he's sitting playing *Call of Duty* pretending to be a soldier killing Afghans and that. I wanted to take the baby away and then come back and pour petrol everywhere and then set fire to them and let them burn.

Beat.

I didn't do any of that though. I didn't say a word and I didn't punch anyone in the face. I just sat and drank my cup of tea which tasted like absolute shit by the way because Lauren never cleans the limescale out of her kettle so it tasted like I had a mouth full of fucking iron.

Sammy   Is that what that is?

Charlie   What?

Sammy   When tea tastes like that.

Charlie   Yeah it's because there's limescale in the kettle.

Sammy   My nan's tea always tastes like it.

Charlie   Tell your mum she needs to get some descaler for your nan's kettle.

Sammy   I will.

Pause.

Charlie   I didn't really want to talk to people anymore. I didn't have anything to say to anyone. I don't like most people I know.

Sammy   I feel like that sometimes.

Charlie   I don't really like people.

Sammy   Me either.

Charlie   Really?

Sammy   Yeah. I think people are nasty to each other all the fucking time.

Charlie   You just battered someone.

Sammy   Because he was nasty. He had no fucking reason to say those things about you to me. He was trying to make pain for no reason and that's what I mean. People have to be protected from that.

Charlie   How do you protect them?

Sammy   Cuddles. I think cuddles are the way forward mate. Cuddles on park benches.

Beat.

What time you got to be in?

Charlie   Whenever, Mum's got bingo tonight.

Sammy   I'll walk you home when you want to go.

She nods.

Silence.

They stay there as 'I'm Forever Blowing Bubbles' sung by Vera Lynn begins.

Lights fade as music continues.

End.